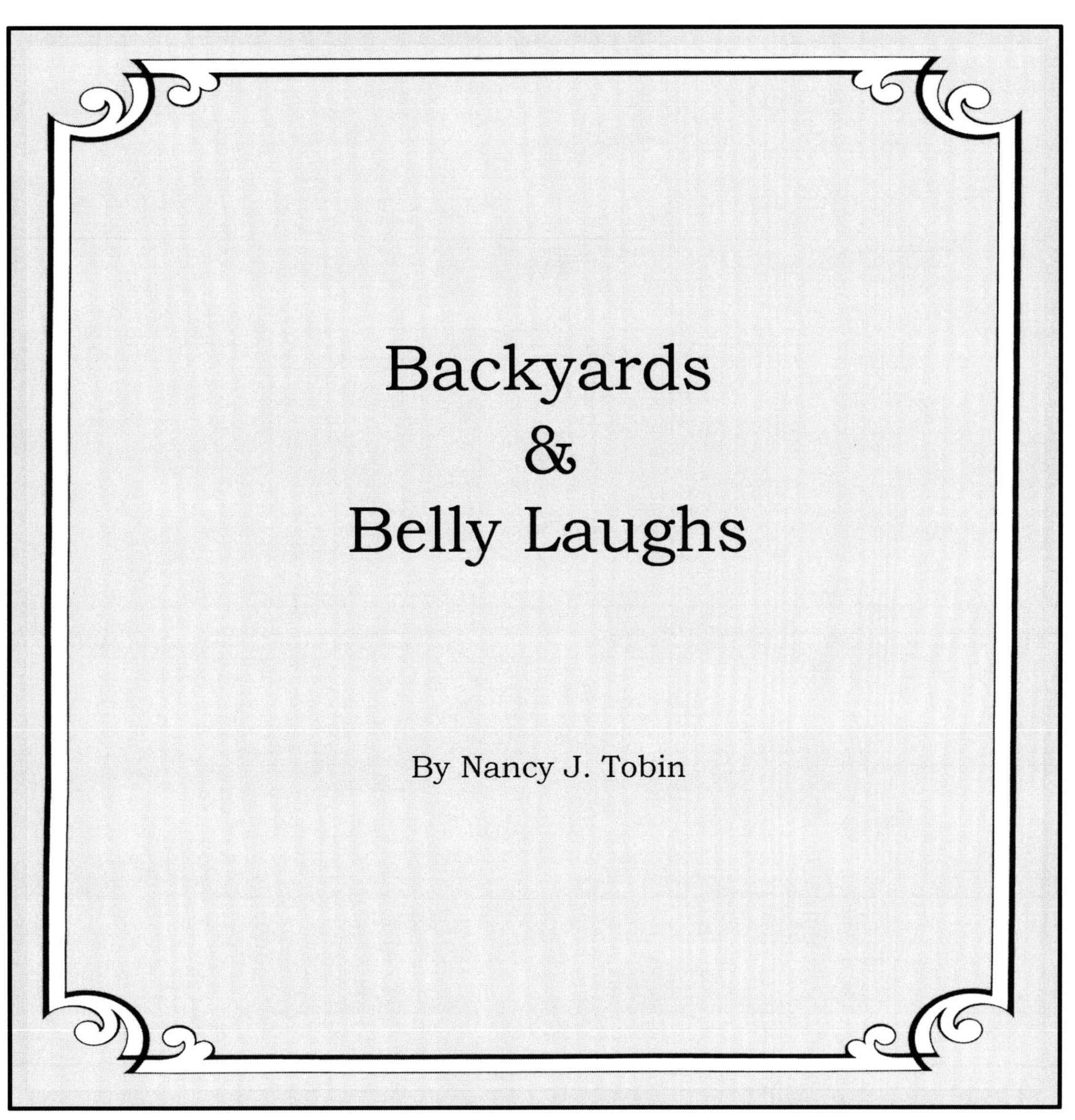

Backyards & Belly Laughs

By Nancy J. Tobin

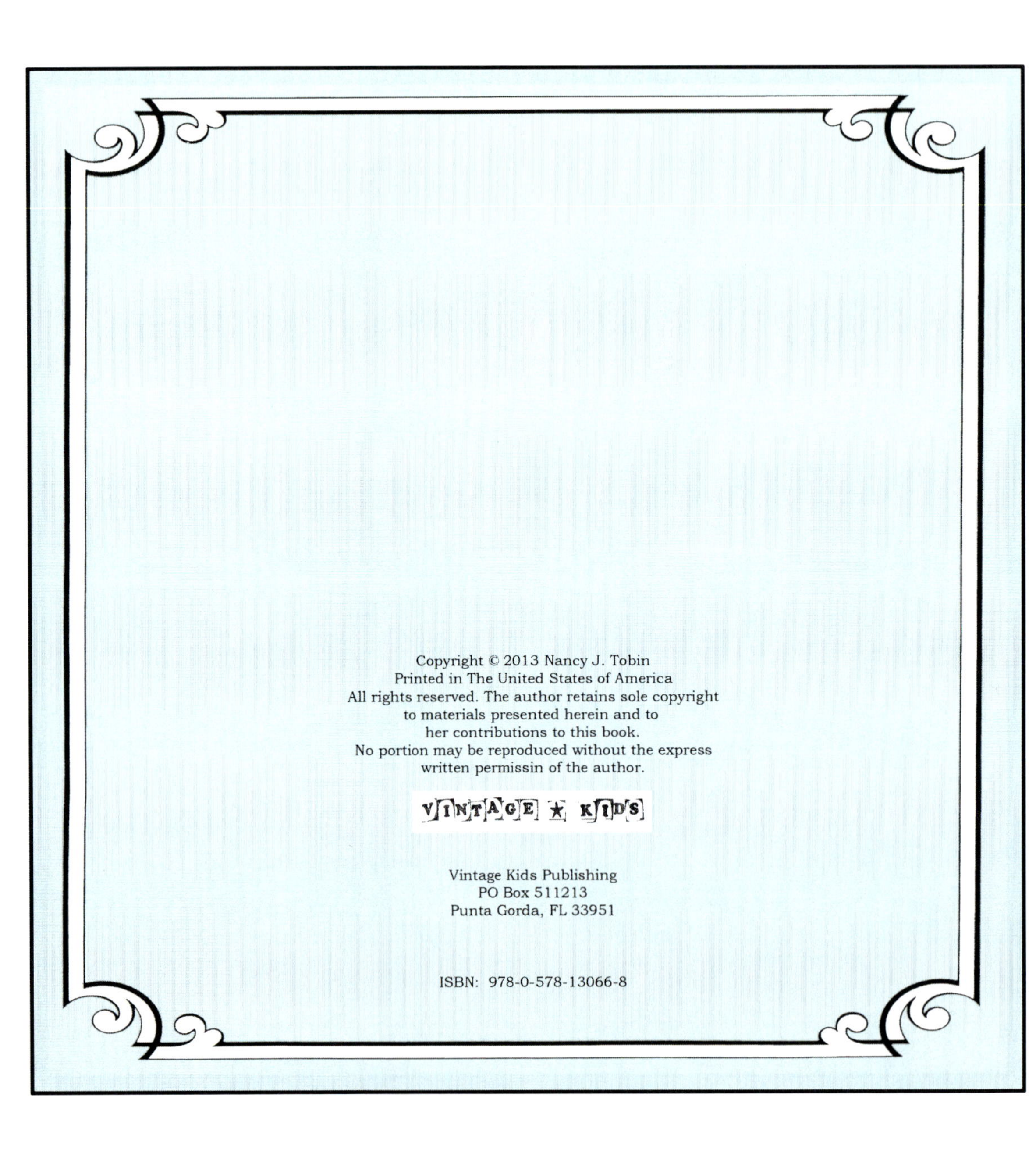

Vintage Kids Publishing
PO Box 511213
Punta Gorda, FL 33951

ISBN: 978-0-578-13066-8

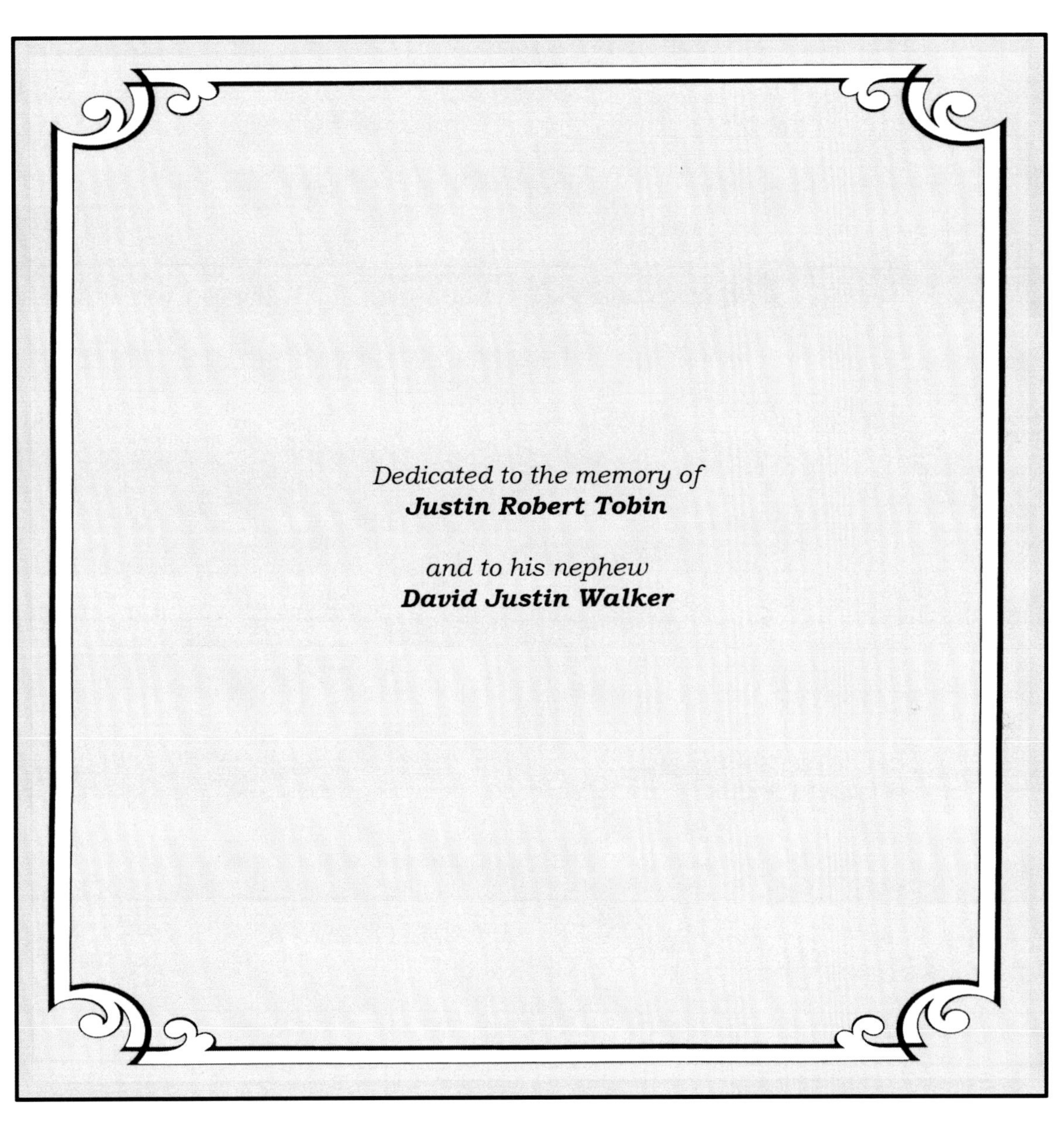

Dedicated to the memory of
Justin Robert Tobin

and to his nephew
David Justin Walker

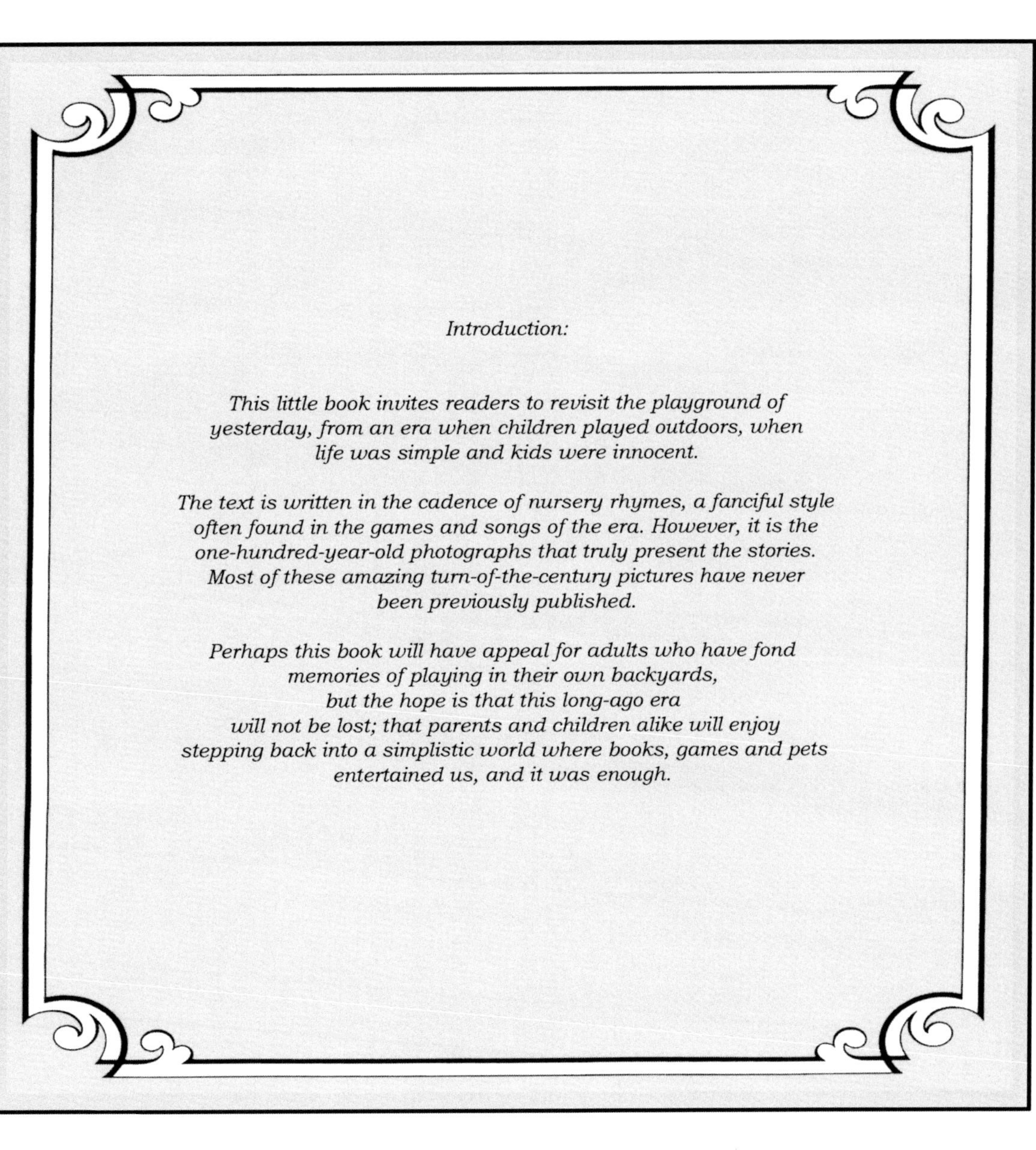

Introduction:

This little book invites readers to revisit the playground of yesterday, from an era when children played outdoors, when life was simple and kids were innocent.

The text is written in the cadence of nursery rhymes, a fanciful style often found in the games and songs of the era. However, it is the one-hundred-year-old photographs that truly present the stories. Most of these amazing turn-of-the-century pictures have never been previously published.

Perhaps this book will have appeal for adults who have fond memories of playing in their own backyards, but the hope is that this long-ago era will not be lost; that parents and children alike will enjoy stepping back into a simplistic world where books, games and pets entertained us, and it was enough.

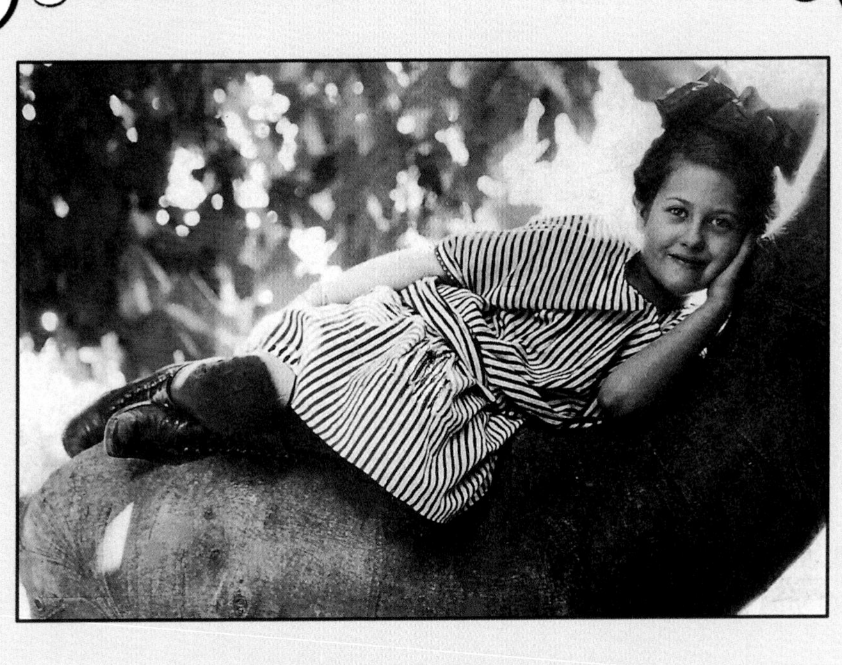

Polly Fulton climbed a tree
with ribbons, bows, and smiles,
all three.

She found a branch to rest a spell
then called to Betty Lou,
"Tell all the boys in the neighborhood
that girls can climb trees too!"

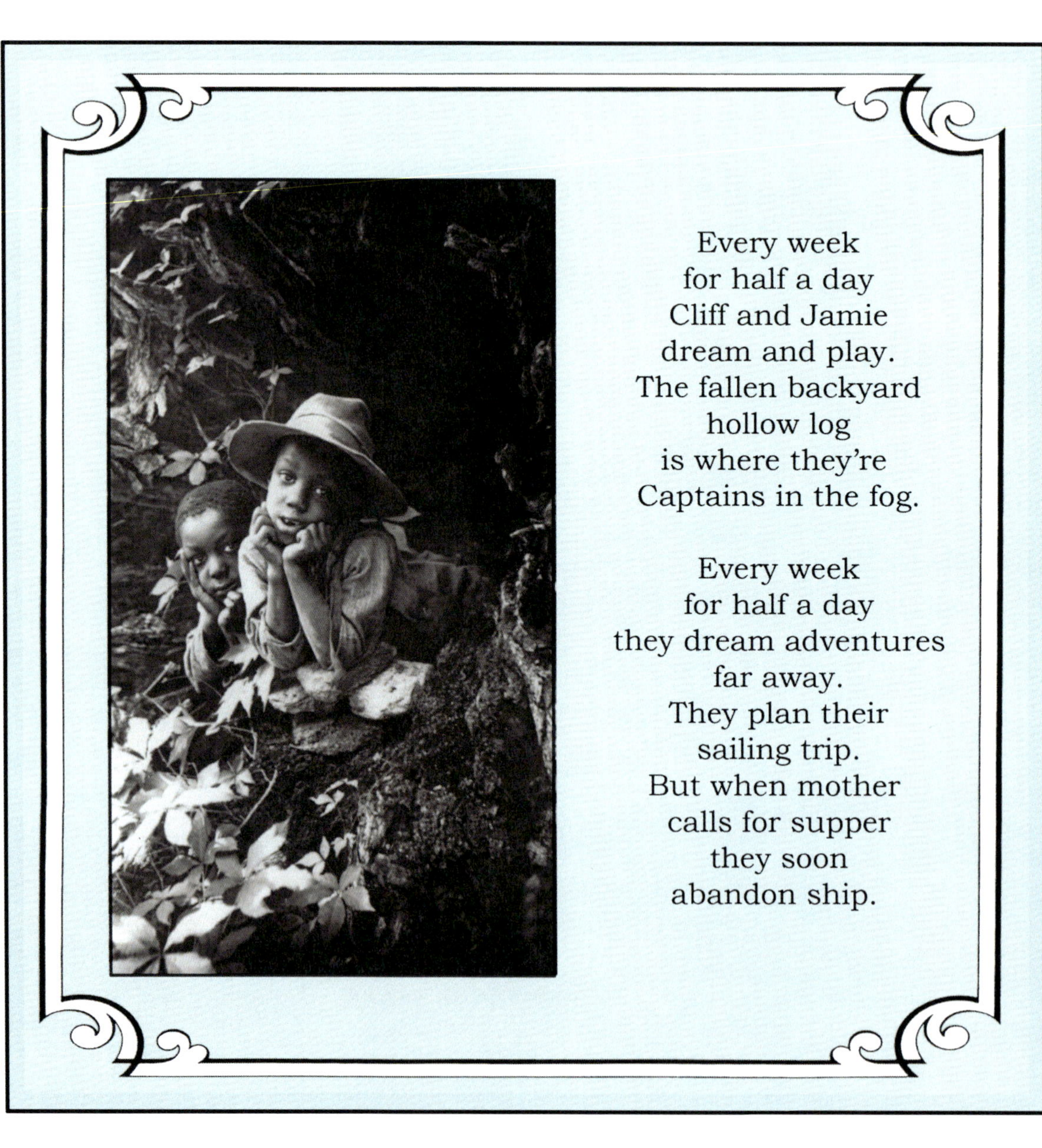

Every week
for half a day
Cliff and Jamie
dream and play.
The fallen backyard
hollow log
is where they're
Captains in the fog.

Every week
for half a day
they dream adventures
far away.
They plan their
sailing trip.
But when mother
calls for supper
they soon
abandon ship.

There is a neighbor
down the lane.
His name is
Henry Hoot.
He rides his mules
while standing up
and in his Sunday suit!

He rode today
down Merry Lane
and when the mules
ran faster,
Henry tumbled
through the air!
'Twas a funny-sad
disaster!

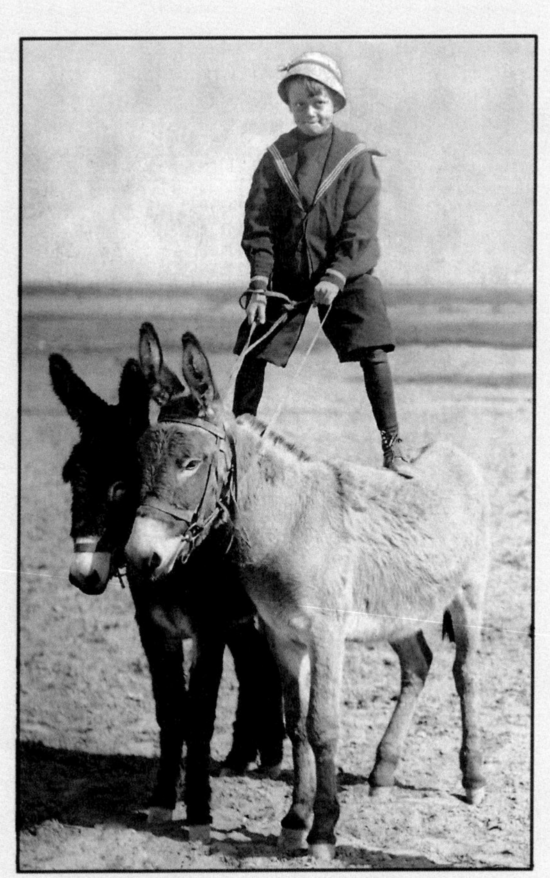

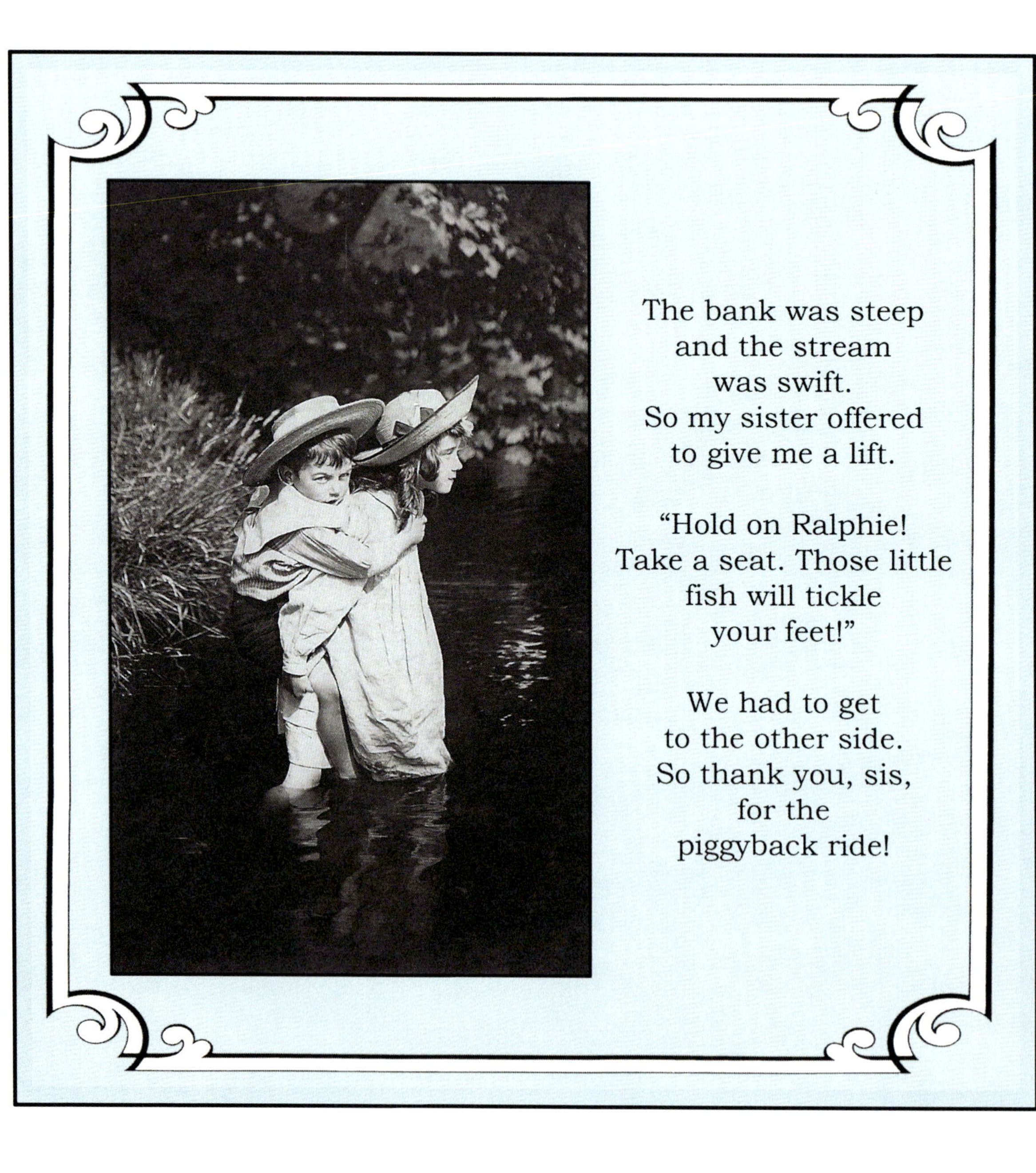

The bank was steep
and the stream
was swift.
So my sister offered
to give me a lift.

"Hold on Ralphie!
Take a seat. Those little
fish will tickle
your feet!"

We had to get
to the other side.
So thank you, sis,
for the
piggyback ride!

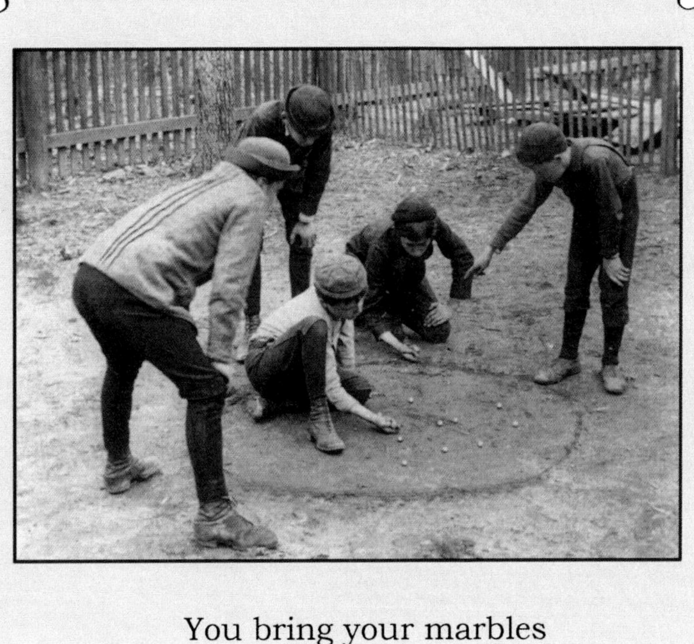

You bring your marbles
and I'll bring mine.
And you can keep my marbles
if they go outside the line.

You draw the "shooters ring"
and I'll "knuckle-down".
Let's play the best Keepsies game
on this side of town.

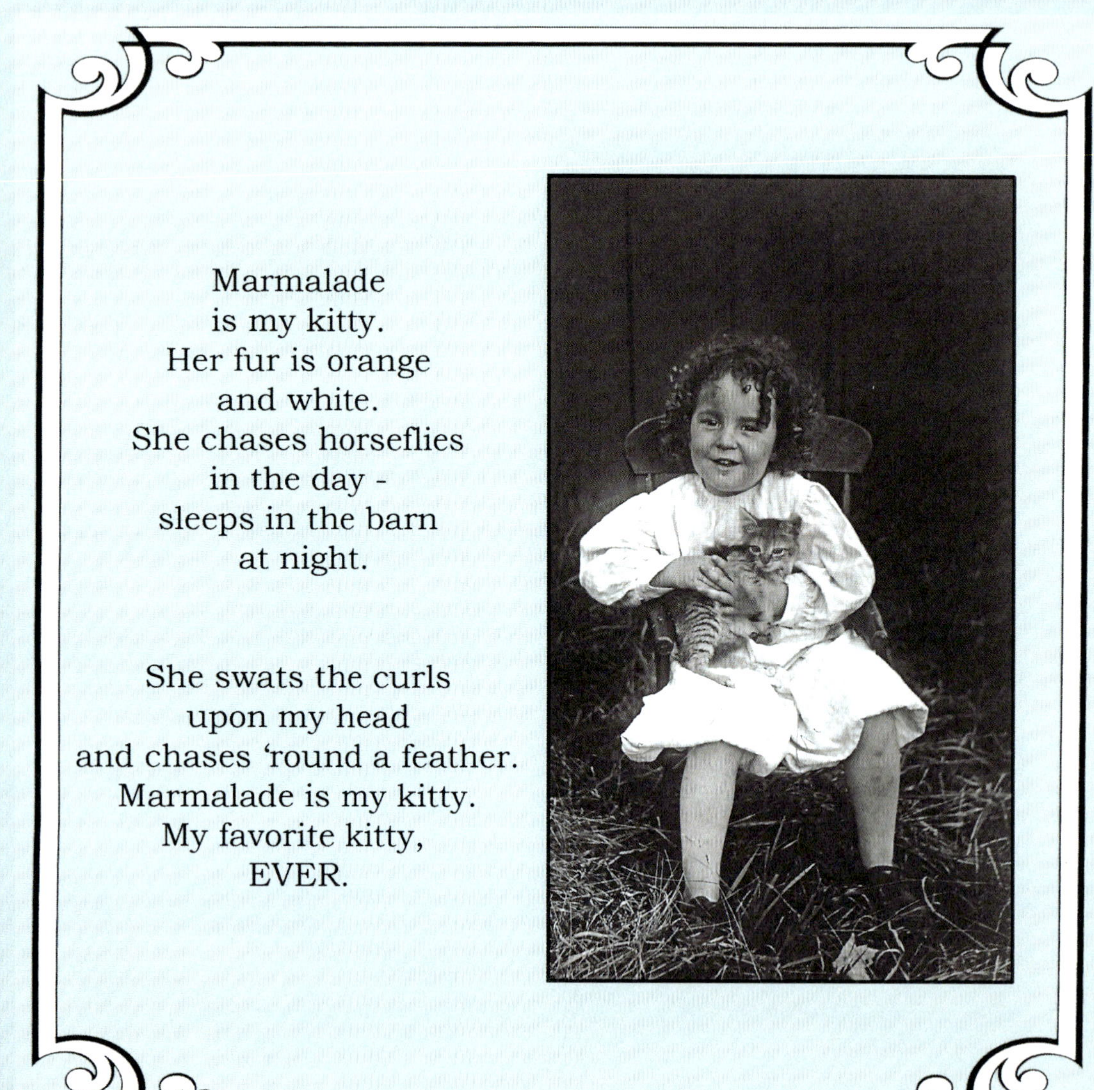

Marmalade
is my kitty.
Her fur is orange
and white.
She chases horseflies
in the day -
- sleeps in the barn
at night.

She swats the curls
upon my head
and chases 'round a feather.
Marmalade is my kitty.
My favorite kitty,
EVER.

Dear Grandma,

Thank you for the
Army doll.
He's handsome as can be.

Grandpa's jacket
that you sewed
fits him perfectly.

He'll be my Army buddy
and secrets we will tell
and when
I grow to be a man
I'll serve my country well.

Love,
Roy

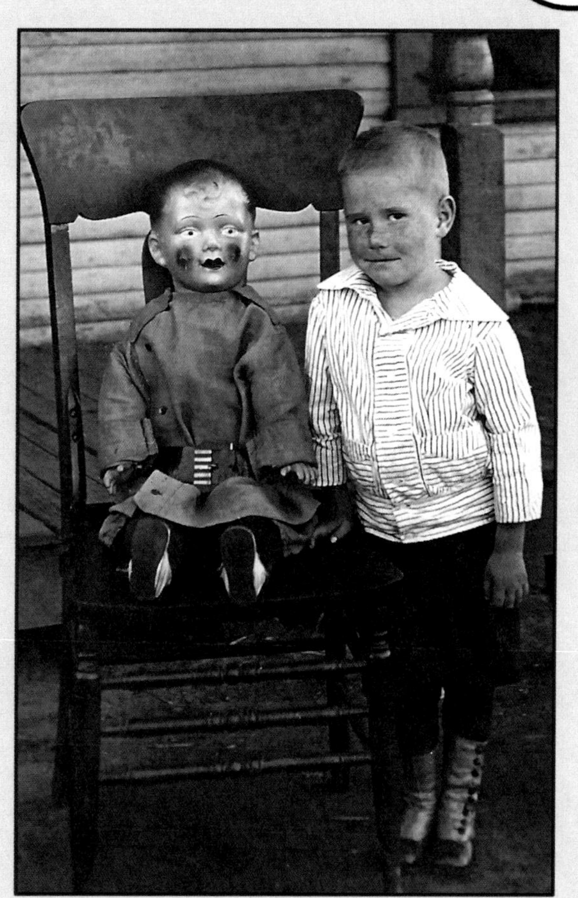

This is my brother.
His name is José
We're going to market.
We go every day.

To the colorful market
and there we will see
the peppers and melons,
the beans, and kiwi.

There's a man
who sells churros
at the end of the day.
He may have a churro
for brother José!

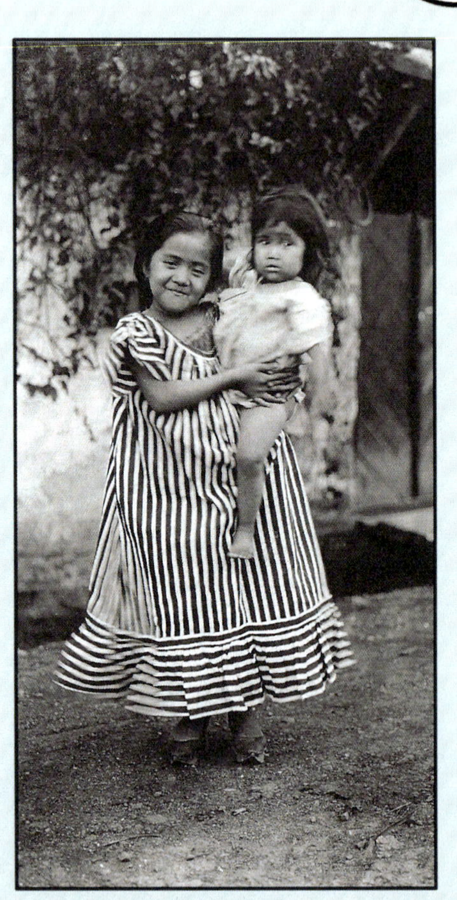

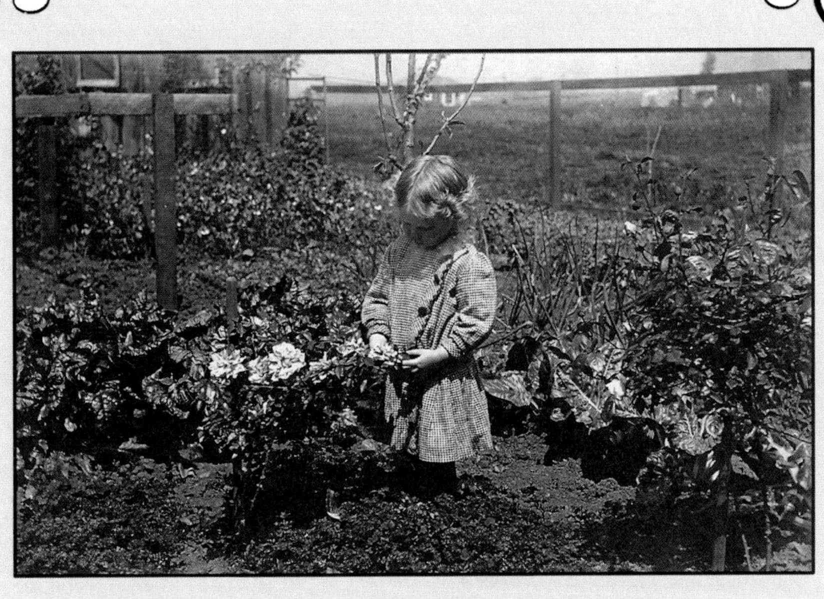

Sarah, Sarah did you know
that *worms* will help your garden grow?

Dig the Earth. Plant a seed.
Wait for rain. Pull a weed.

Mother Nature always knows
where something beautiful will grow.

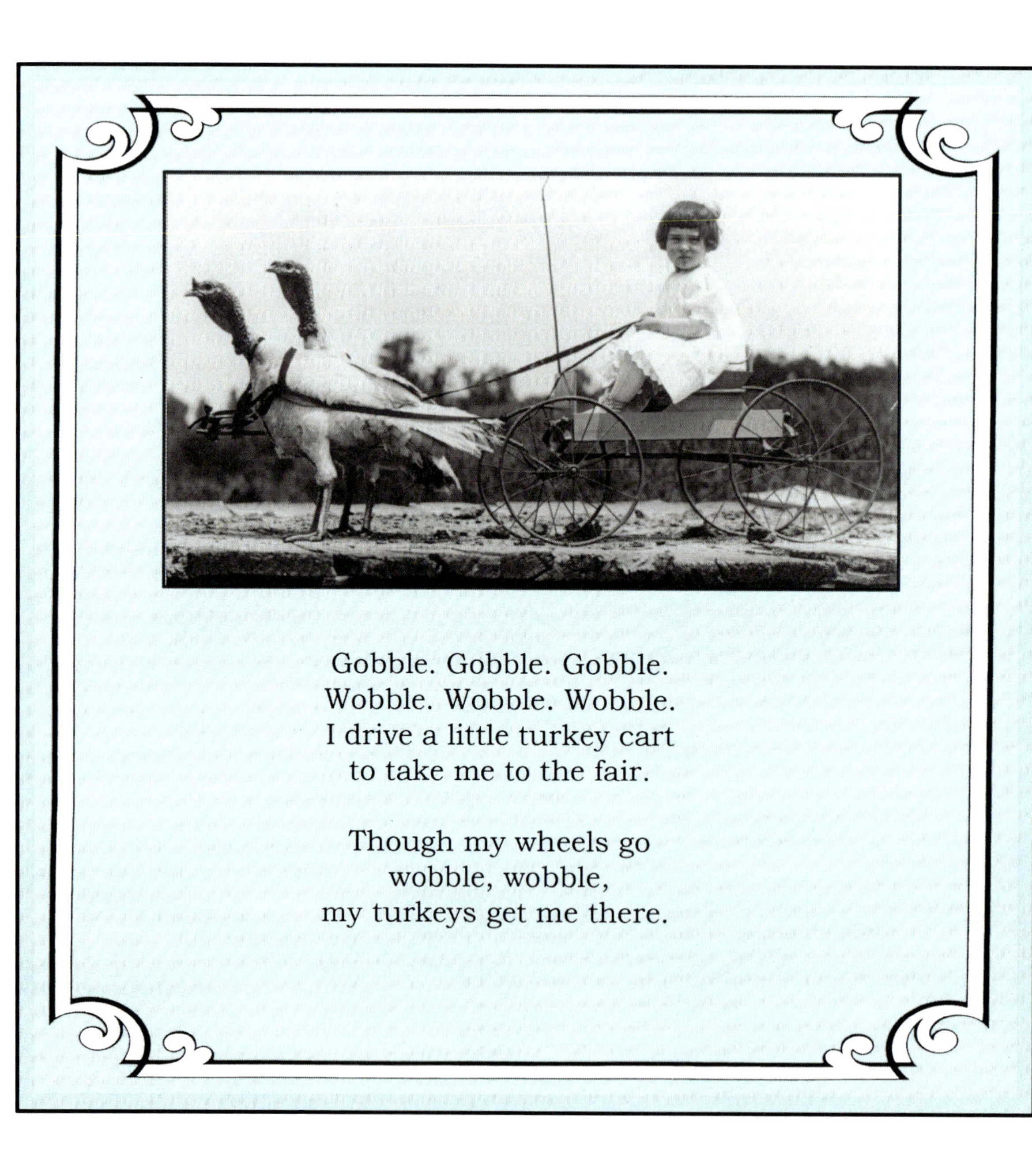

Gobble. Gobble. Gobble.
Wobble. Wobble. Wobble.
I drive a little turkey cart
to take me to the fair.

Though my wheels go
wobble, wobble,
my turkeys get me there.

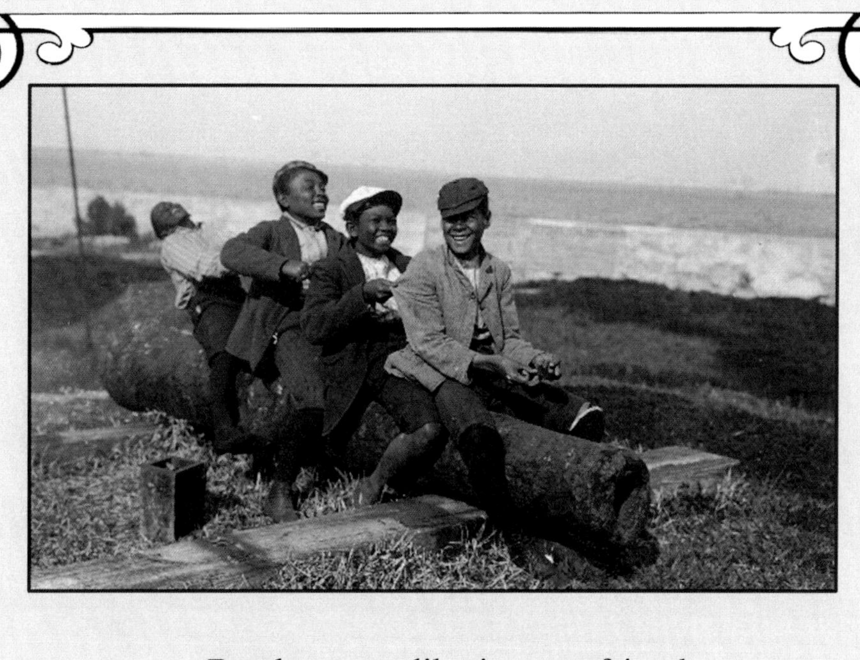

Brothers are like instant friends.
When there's nothing else to do,
you can always ask your brother
to come along with you.

Having brothers always means
acting crazy, laughing,
screams.

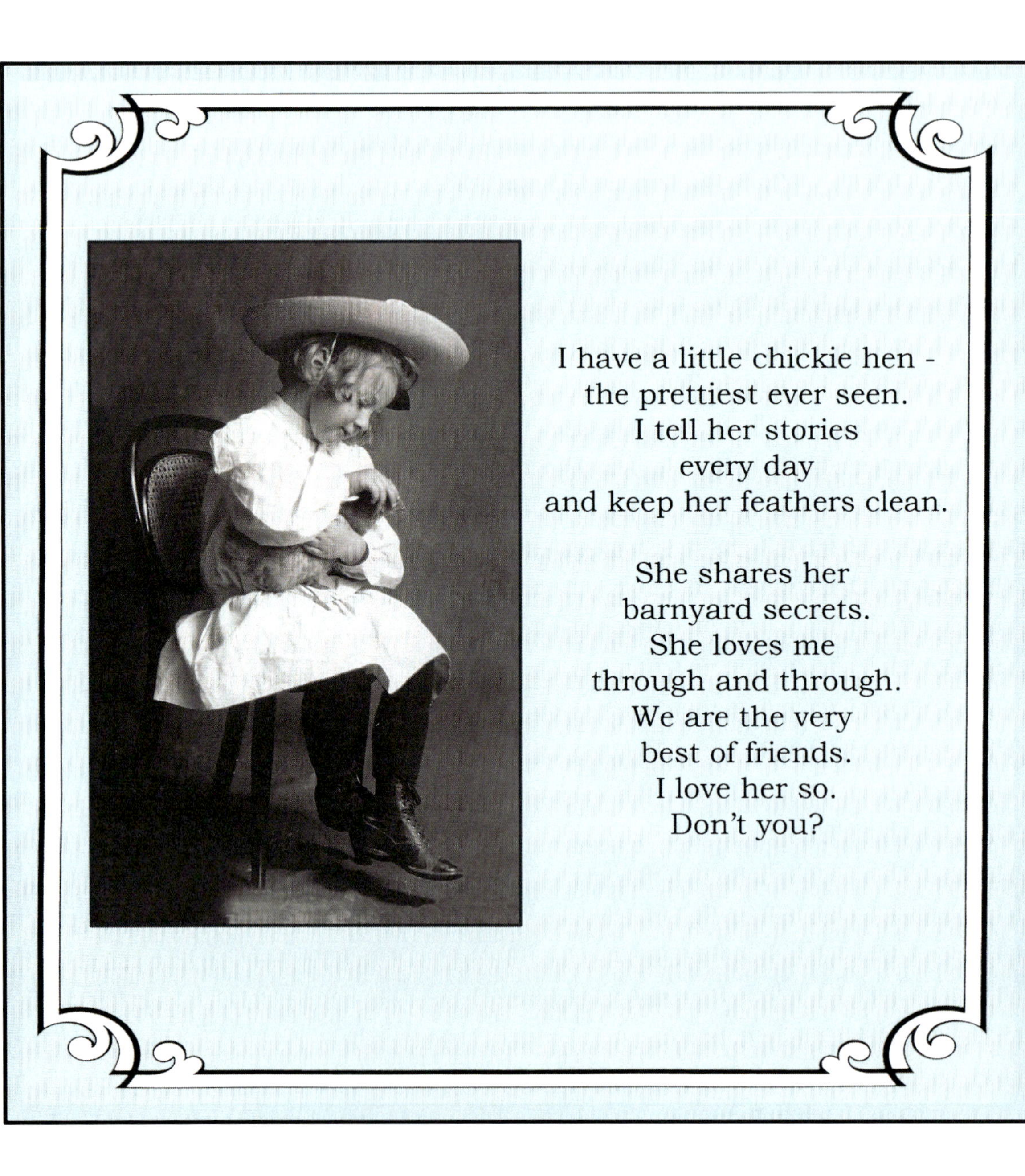

I have a little chickie hen -
the prettiest ever seen.
I tell her stories
every day
and keep her feathers clean.

She shares her
barnyard secrets.
She loves me
through and through.
We are the very
best of friends.
I love her so.
Don't you?

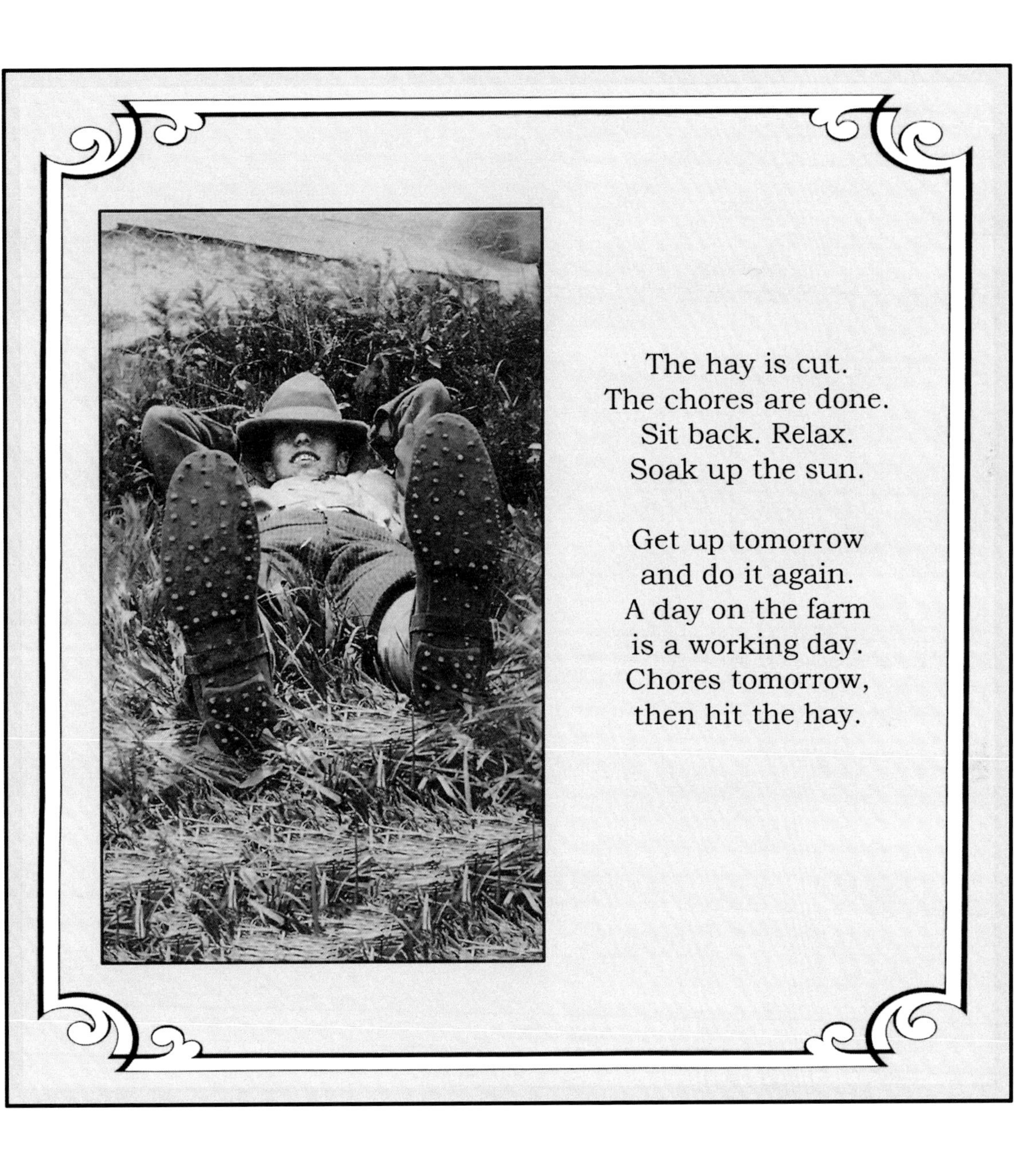

The hay is cut.
The chores are done.
Sit back. Relax.
Soak up the sun.

Get up tomorrow
and do it again.
A day on the farm
is a working day.
Chores tomorrow,
then hit the hay.

Sometimes
when I'm naughty
my Mama makes me sit
to think about the things
I've done
so all the bad will quit.

Boo, my dog,
sits with me too
and knows just what to do.
Pretty posies for my 'Ma
will make her smile.
Boo knew.

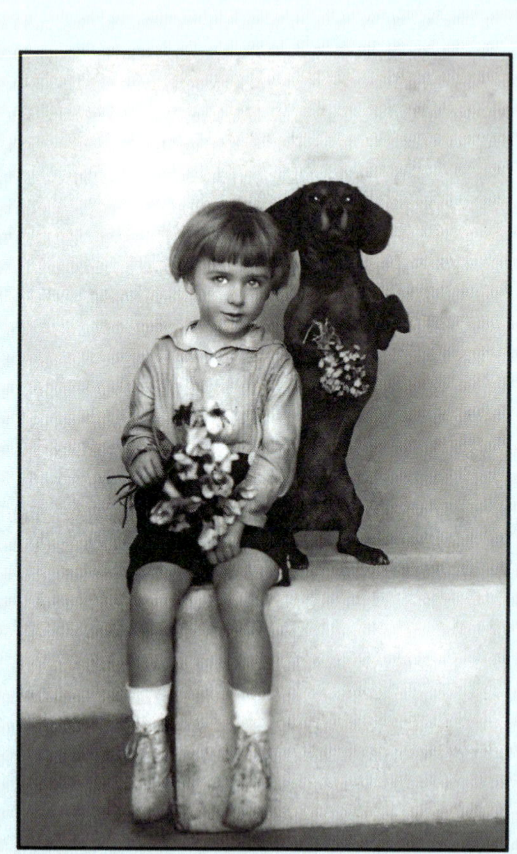

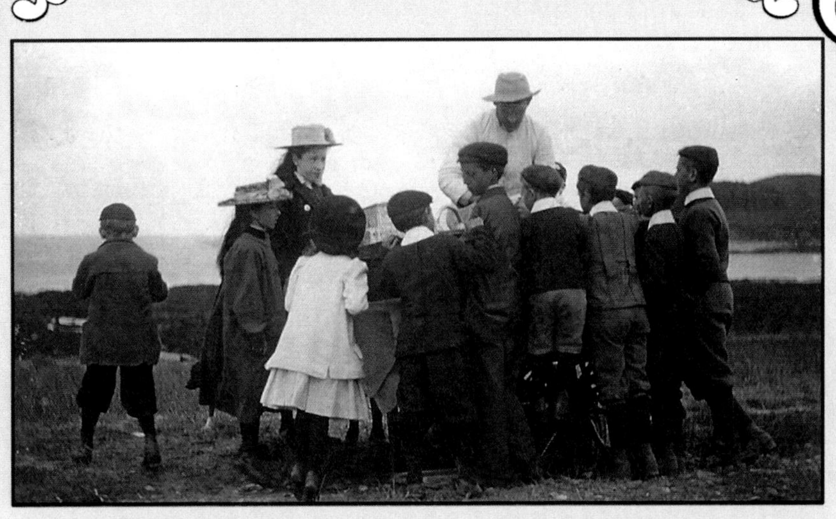

Hurry. Hurry,
as fast as you can.
Bring your nickel
for the ice cream man.

The ice cream man
is playing his song
Hurry. Hurry.
Hurry along.

Line up boys.
Line up girls.
Vanilla. Chocolate.
And even swirls.

The ice cream man
is ready to churn.
Hurry. Hurry.
But wait your turn.

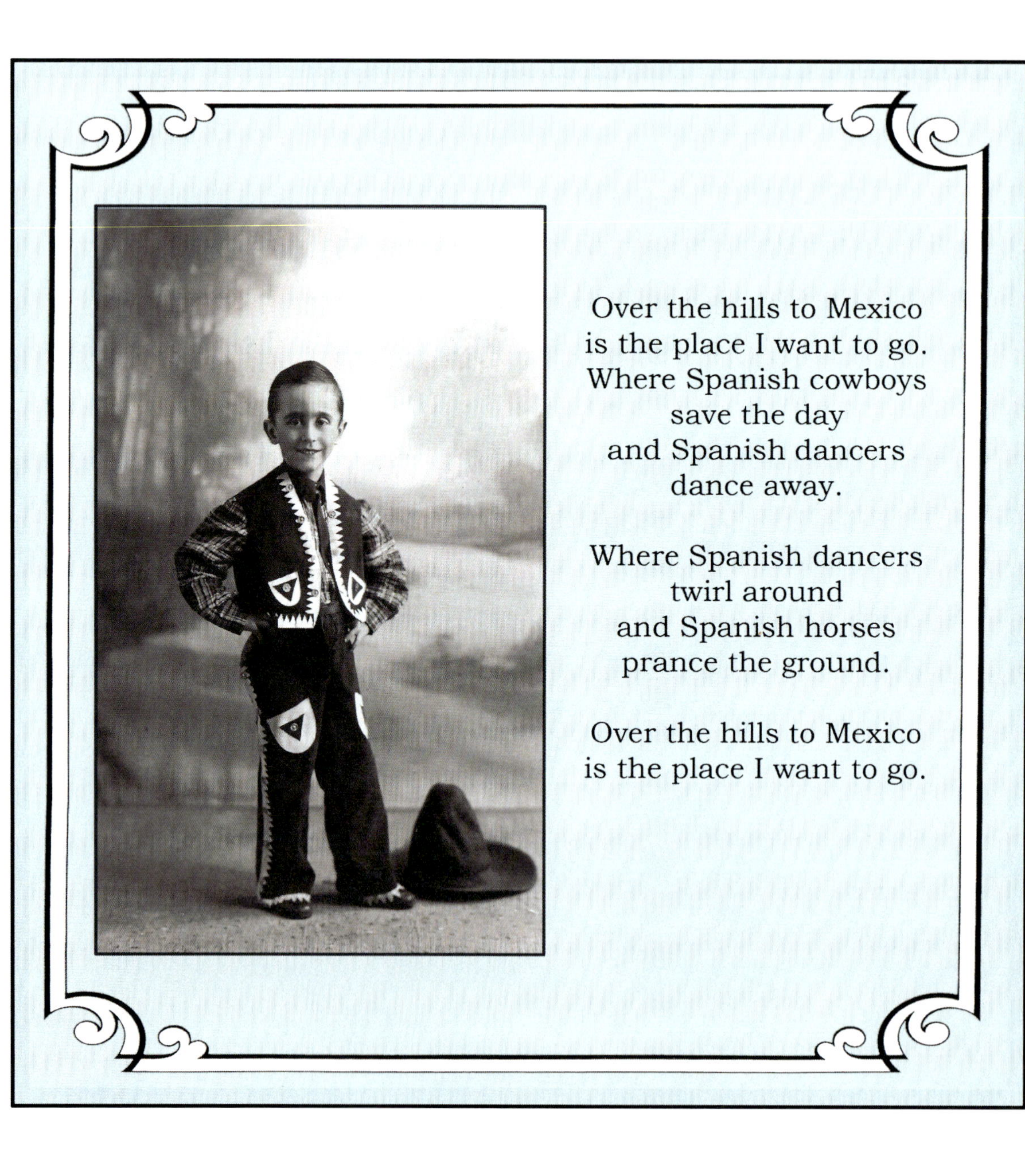

Over the hills to Mexico
is the place I want to go.
Where Spanish cowboys
save the day
and Spanish dancers
dance away.

Where Spanish dancers
twirl around
and Spanish horses
prance the ground.

Over the hills to Mexico
is the place I want to go.

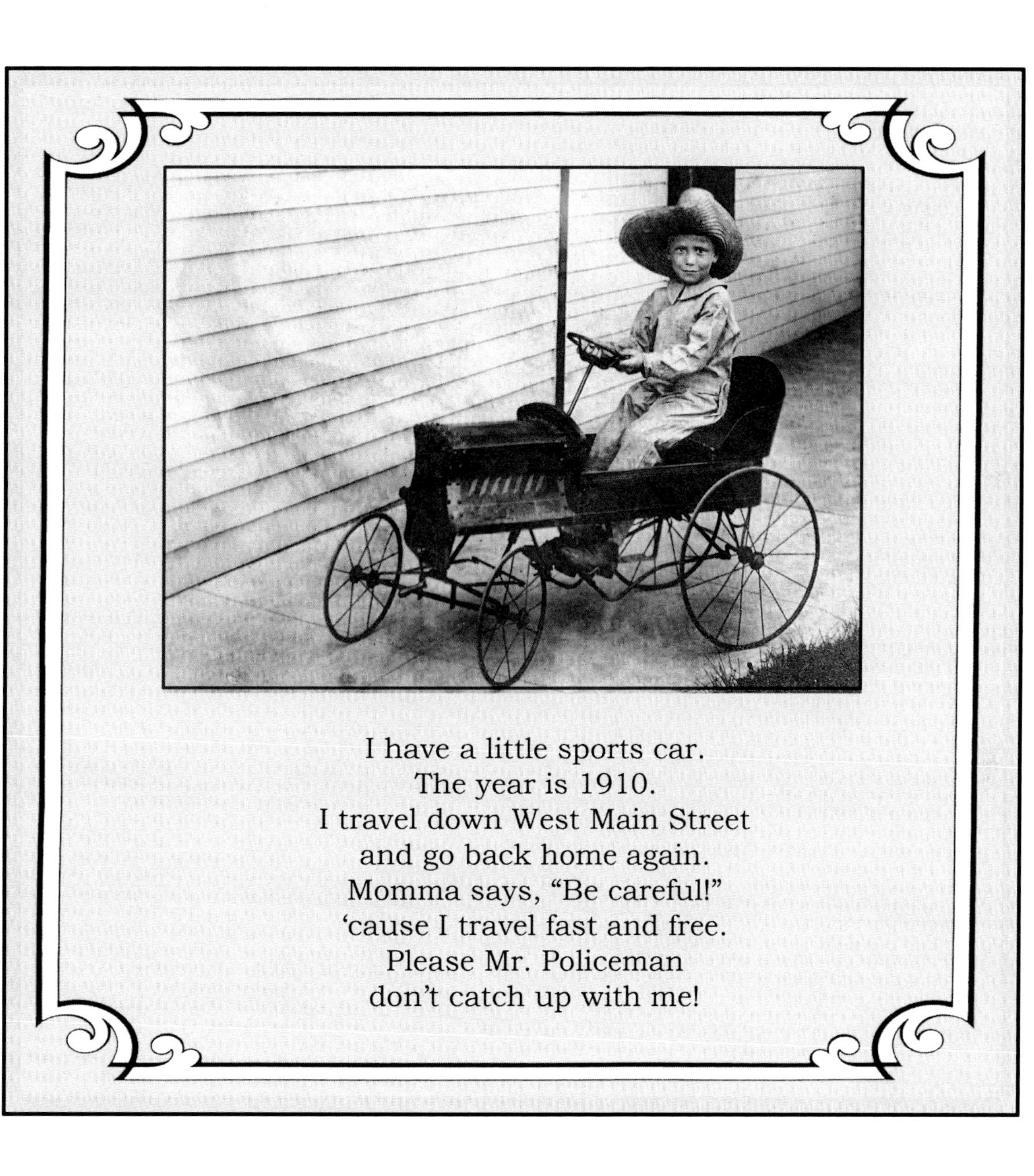

I have a little sports car.
The year is 1910.
I travel down West Main Street
and go back home again.
Momma says, “Be careful!”
‘cause I travel fast and free.
Please Mr. Policeman
don’t catch up with me!

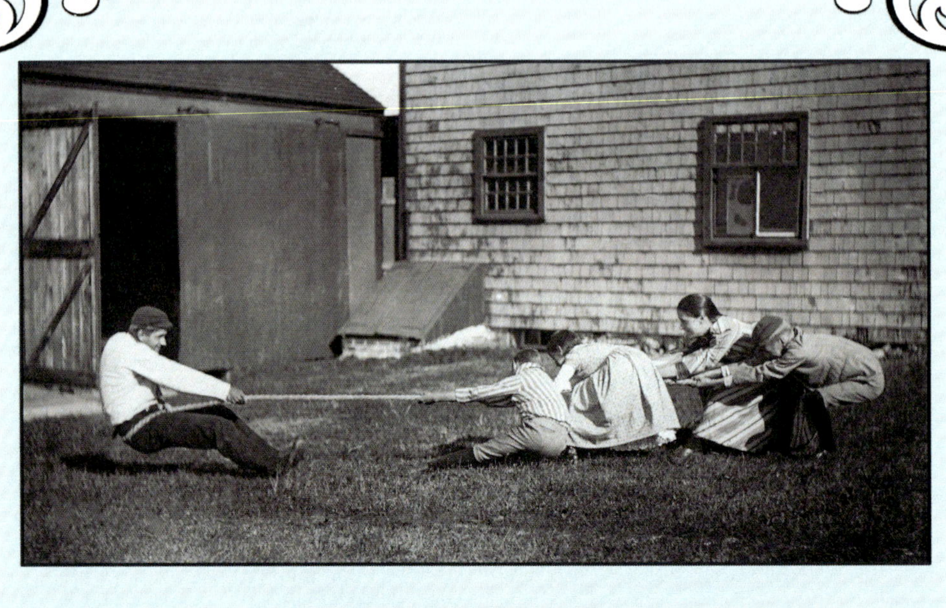

Tug. Tug. Pull. Pull.
Four against one is the rule.
We can win. We always do.

We know we're kids
but we are strong.
Keep on p-u-l-l-i-n-g...
'Til Pa gets a hitch in his get-along.

Photo Credits and Information:

Key: RPPC=Real Photo Post Card; AC=authors collection; LOC=Library of Congress Prints & Photographs Division; All images circa:1895-1915.

COVER: Design by Baumgartner Design, Poulsbo, WA, www.baumgartner-design.com;

Cliff and Jamie: LOC, c. 1895; Polly Fulton: RPPC, AC; Henry Hoot:RPPC, AC; Piggyback Ride: RPPC, AC; Keepsies: LOC; Marmalade: RPPC, AC; Army Doll: RPPC, AC; Brother Jose: RPPC, AC; Sarah, Sarah: RPPC, AC; Turkey Cart: LOC; Brothers: LOC; Chickie Hen: Cabinet Card, circa:1895, AC; Hit the Hay: RPPC, c.1906, AC; Boo & Posies: RPPC, AC; Ice Cream Man: antique print, AC; Spanish Dancers: RPPC, AC; Sports Car: RPPC, AC; Tug-o-War: 5 x7 antique print, AC

~~~

All available information for these photos is given above. Names used in the poems are fictitious. Attempts have been made at further identification, however most were personal family photos with no caption, names, or locations. Photo manipulation may have been used to improve quality.
~~~

CPSIA information can be obtained
at www.ICGtesting.com
Printed in the USA
LVXC01n0949091213
364258LV00005B/4